THE WINNING CAPTAIN

HOW SOURAV GANGULY PLAYED HIS WAY

BY

ANANYA BHANJA CHAUDHURI

Dada's journey on and off cricket field

Unveil the core strategies that will change your life and bring about a better you

<u>COPYRIGHT</u>

Copyright @ 2020 by Ananya Bhanja Chaudhuri

DEDICATION

To,

Author & Poet Nandita Daniel (My Masi) for shaping my

dream for writing non-fiction book into reality;

Sikha Bhanja Chaudhuri (My mother) for being my constant

source of inspiration;

All the Sourav Ganguly fans across the globe for whom the

beautiful game of cricket is more than just a game but a

universal emotion of unity and aggression in the face of crisis

or hindrance.

"Yeh toh sirf aagaaz hain, shuruaat hai safar ka

Mein nehi koi yoddha, lekin meri kalam hi auzaar hain"

-    Ananya Bhanja Chaudhuri

TABLE OF CONTENTS

ABOUT THE AUTHOR

Ananya Bhanja Chaudhuri was born in Kolkata and brought up in Durgapur, West Bengal, India. For her higher studies, she shifted back to her roots in Kolkata. She has done MA (Political Science from Calcutta University) and PGDM (Advertising and Marketing from Bharatiya Vidya Bhavan). For the last fifteen years, she had been juggling between her professional like Creative Head of an Educational Organisation and her passion for Writing and Filmmaking. She is a perfect multitasker and a dynamic individual. She is also an avid reader. She is also interested in politics, movies especially classics, and sketching whenever she gets time. Belonging to the same city as Dada, she has a passion for Cricket and the love for the game took her to write this book.

ABOUT THE BOOK

This is not essentially a biography book on Sourav Ganguly. Readers will get a glimpse of his life through his ups and downs. Also, there are certain learning from each chapter that will motivate you all. Each chapter focuses on how driven Ganguly was and how to go ahead in our life following those principles.

So, this is essential for all readers across the globe who not only love sports but also want to feel determined at each point of crisis in their life. You could be a student, a homemaker, or a corporate person, you always go through some amount of humiliation or constraint in your daily life. I have provided some hacks to handle such situations.

I have seen my friends suffer in their life and as they don't know the way out, often then resort to extreme life risky measures. Life is most precious as its God gifted. As such we should get on with it with full positivity amid oppositions. That's what we draw out of Ganguly's life.

I took a lesson from this, I went ahead and started to write this book. And while researching through the online medium I have felt a transition in myself. My life had gone totally upside down, and now I know it's my responsibility to shed light on people to motivate and inspire all the more.

Well what more, read the book and know more.

Happy Reading.

ACKNOWLEDGEMENTS

Thank you readers and friends for picking up two books written earlier. This has given the impetus to go ahead and write this book.

This is my first non-fictional book. And while writing this book especially in this genre I often fall short of work and thought impossible for me to continue. It was in such moments my Masi, Nandita Daniel inspired me to get through with it.

Writing about an iconic figure like Sourav Ganguly was an inevitable choice but the real suggestion came from my mother. She often says if you write, then write to inspire. She created the perfect ambiance for writing in between the daily mundane of life. She made sure that I complete it that too before my birthday i.e., 8th September so that I can treat myself with the same.

I also thank my colleague and friend Amrita Mallick who pushed me ahead in the publication procedure which initially seemed tough to achieve.

<u>1</u>

<u>NATION'S BELOVED DADA</u>

"There is no substitute for hard work" - Thomas A. Edison

Learning the Lesson of Perseverance & Self Belief

Cricket has gone through a transformation over the years. But for cricket lovers, Sourav Ganguly will always remain as a national sentiment. Sourav Ganguly, compassionately known as 'Dada' of the nation will always remain as the true leader who helped his successors to become leaders in their later years. He backed up his players exceptionally, which is considered as most important in modern-day captaincy. He is a real Hero, an aggressive Guide, and a hardworking Teacher who saw the potential of his team in the midst of controversies and turned around the wheel in their favor. He showed us that if you have the potential, no hindrance can stop you from achieving your goal. He was a Champion of Champions who gave us the direction on how to remain driven towards your goals in life.

He taught us the way to stay calm and remain focused within the middle of a storm. It had been the time when national dailies were regularly publishing articles and accusing prominent players of match-fixing, he kept the fighting spirit alive in his team and made them specialise in cricket only. So thousands of hindrance may come your way, never leave your goal only to flee the wrath of others.

Nation's sentiment is still very much attached to his name even though he retired in 2008. How he led his life, how he played for India is a learning lesson for millions across borders. He created an era, wherein a bunch of youths found their goals in front of them.

Now think of yourself, who always blamed the others who had never treated you well or didn't accepted you or recognized your true potential. So you had been procrastinating your desires all this time in the fear of failure. Here is one man, whose journey can motivate you out of your fear psychosis and strive for fulfilling your dreams which you have been holding back for ages. I am not a cricketer, I remember the day when he announced his retirement in a press conference, how the entire nation mourned, and I was not an exception. Though he retired from the international cricket periphery, he was remained always glued to the sports. He tried his best, to bring the talents to the forefront through sports. Even today, he is doing a great job as the President of the Cricket Association of Bengal (C.A.B), improving the quality of the Eden Gardens stadium, and trying to develop young talents from Bengal with projects like "Vision 2020".

This is the lesson we learned, whatever you do, make a mark, create an aura around you and let others follow. There are such situations in corporate life, when companies are facing a huge crisis that's the time a leader keeps the employees together, motivates them and keep their integrity intact to the organization. Trust and loyalty to a leader is phenomenal, see the case of a homemaker. Sikha, my mother got married early in her life. She knew nothing as to how to run a household. Like a bird's nest, she added one after one straw of her hardship that made her a confident woman of today. She is that lady, who everyone's favorite not just in the house but through social media. It's just that you have to act and stop procrastinating because tomorrow never comes.

Now, let's keep it between you and me. Do you fear of something? Is your fear stopping you to take up any decision or action? Then break out of it. Take the pressure off from your shoulder. Let me give you my example. When initially I started writing, I felt tremendous pressure because I feared if I could meet the deadline especially when the topic was so new to me. And then the best thing I could do is I took a short break or perhaps a cheat break. Yes, a cheat break!! I didn't let others know that I am not working, and instead, I made small refreshment relief by watching sports videos or motivating interviews of Sourav Ganguly. So I hit the bull's-eye by watching something of importance and added to my research also, while on the other hand, I found it so relaxing.

Sourav Ganguly, himself once said he never cried in his life. Failures did affect him, but he never took resort to tears which seemed to be an easy escape. He is that man, who followed his principles and kept his self-belief intact even when he was falling. Centuries after centuries he had made at the test cricket but it seemed never enough to please the selectors. Was there any hidden agenda behind this ignorance, we don't know. But we know one thing, Ganguly fought it hard, he fought it right.

When you are in charge of something you must not hide behind the bushes. Rather have the courage to stand tall and use your communication skills to grab the attention of others. Even today when we see Dada in the Zee Bangla Episode of Dadagiri, he sets the stage on fire. Eyewitnesses confirmed, the moment he enters the set of the show there is positive energy flowing throughout. He not only keeps the ambiance comfortable for participants, he listens to them which is an integral part of communication.

And added to it his simplicity and that smile on his face make our heart melt. A great son and brother, a loving husband, and caring father- this is something that is integral to his name. Dona Ganguly whom he often calls as Madam said in an interview recently that if Sourav comes to politics he will excel in any case. His 18 years old daughter Sana Ganguly, is also very proud of her father, as she says the way to go to him when she got trolled for the wrong reason and her father went ahead to safeguard the family's image.

So, what we get is that life is not that easy. Thousands and thousands of hurdles will come your way. Each day something new will crop up. What you do, think like Sourav, and Be like Sourav and trigger the success button till you reach the summit of success. That's it, just get to work and stay focused as this will enable you to surmount unknown hurdles. And always remember to plan your actions well in advance to face unforeseen hardships. This not only keeps you strong but your team remains integrated in the time of need. Then together you can face the storm, which becomes much casy to handle. Obviously, Ganguly knew this from the very beginning, that's why he could strategize so well in the ODIs. The unbeatable record at the Lords was his answer to those who were apprehensive about his ability.

<u>2</u>

<u>A WONDER KID WAS BORN</u>

"You are unique. You have different talents and abilities. You don't have to always follow in the footsteps of others. And most important, you should always remind yourself that you don't have to do what everyone else is doing and have a responsibility to develop the talents you have been given".

- Roy T, Bennett

Decoding his childhood days

Born on 8th July 1972 in Kolkata, he was the second son of his father, Chandidas Ganguly, and mother, Nirupa

Ganguly. He was the pampered junior brother of Snehashish Ganguly. They had a rich household backed by a flourishing printing business. Sourav Ganguly was growing up in a protected ambiance in his household. Little they had known that he would become world-famous someday. Those days, cricket was not a popular sport in the domestic arena, rather football was everyone's favorite. Like every kid, Sourav had a keen interest in football. But it was his elder brother, who was then a stable cricketer from Bengal, introduced him to the 22 yards and from there the passion grew.

Soon he took admission in a cricket academy wherein the coach first noticed his talent in batting. He grew up and so is his passion for cricket kept growing. He learned the intricacies of the sports along with his brother. He was still in his school years when he scored a century for Orissa Under-15 and became the captain of the St. Xavier School's cricket team.

Another lesson we can draw from here is how your child is growing up to be determined by his peers. Today's kids are often kept locked inside their homes stuck between their heavy piles of books. The overprotected, over-ambitious parents, fail to look into the eyes of the kids and see through his dreams. These kids often grow up to be less attentive, who resort to hiding behind others. They never become a confident individual, and fail to lead. The parents need to identify the children's strengths and help them nurture that. They should never poke on their weaknesses, rather help them improve on those. Parents, just stop being decisive in terms of your kids. Communicate, communicate, and communicate with your kids. Don't forget there is even a lot more to learn from them because they are generation next. Don't damage their future in the name of care. Kids get suffocated because of this. Foster your kid's independence in all phases of their life.

Ganguly even today's talks of his family support in building his cricket career. In 1989 he got selected to play in the Bengal team. By coincidence Snehashish Ganguly, the elder brother dropped from the side that year. He made a great impression in the 1990-91 season of Ranji Trophy and emerged into the forefront. That marked the beginning of an era of the left-hander. He entered the international cricket arena in 1992 with his debut in ODI again West Indies. But he could not do well in his match and dropped from the team. He was perceived to be arrogant and his attitude towards cricket was questioned at the most. With sheer determination, he returned with more vigor in the team after four years owing to his excellent domestic cricket performances.

Sourav Ganguly played an excellent 131-run knock in his Test debut against England and reckoned as the third cricketer after Harry Graham and John Hampshire to score a century at Lord's in their debut match. The next Test match with his deadly partnership with Sachin Tendulkar broke all records to share a 255 –run opening and having s knock of 136 runs. That test had ended in a draw, heading England ahead at 1-0 series victory, where Ganguly scored 48 in the second innings.

The year 1997 was remarkable for Sourav Ganguly for many reasons. That year, Sourav took a difficult step in his personal life. He eloped with childhood sweet Dona Roy because both the families were against their alliance. Later they came to understanding and reconciliation and the two got officially married in February that year. The wedding worked like a magic for his career. Same year Sourav Ganguly opened the Indian innings against Sri Lanka to score his outstanding 11-run knock which was his first ODI century. And that paved the way to his sensational international cricket career.

Often called Prince of Kolkata, as the name given by Geoffrey Boycott reached new heights of success in his coming years and made us proud as Bengalis across the world. Thus we can draw from here that a leader doesn't bear but they evolve with time. Later years he faced immense hindrance but growing controversies made him more strong and matured. While climbing the corporate ladder, this is what is expected from you. Learn it now like never.

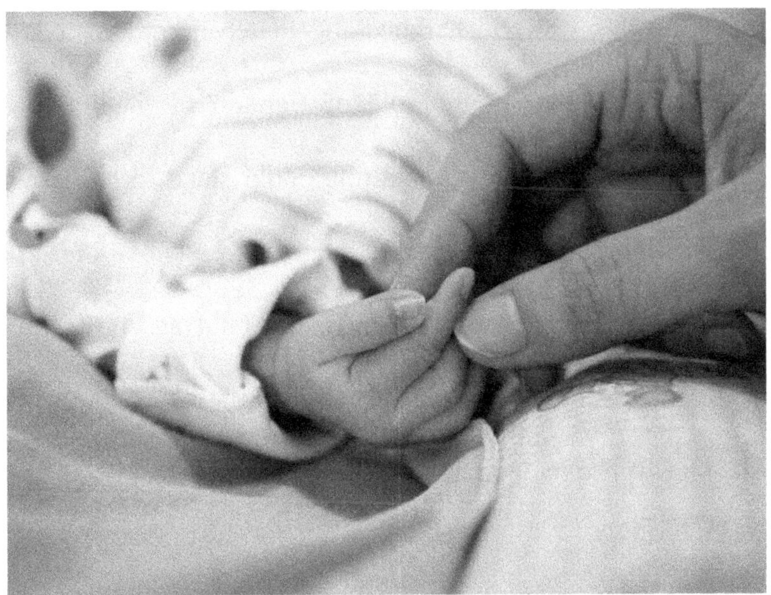

I know people often say that he or she is a born talent. That is simply not true. We are gifted but if we don't nurture them, never will flourish or succeed in life. The amazing man of high principles, Sourav Ganguly, never for a moment was drifted apart and felt demotivated. Yes, there were moments of dissatisfaction and disturbances in his life, which he knew will pass if he remains calm, strategic, and hardworking and true to his countrymen.

See this how he handled the match-fixing scandal, and how he diluted in the role of Captain of the Indian Cricket Team. Nothing, just nothing could stand in his way when the motivated his team to play aggressively for the nation. When India beat England in the ODI at Lord's he swayed his T-Shirt from the balcony of the Lord's was a perfect answer to the opponents.

That's how you should play and that's how you should fight. Sourav Ganguly is still very fond of his memory at Lords. Recently he had visited the same balcony and took a selfie reliving the iconic moment. Ganguly, who is commentating during the India-England ongoing series, had visited the Lord's Cricket Ground and when he arrived at the famous balcony. He shared the picture on Twitter also. It proves efforts never go in vain. If he had lost hope in facing any challenge, we would have missed a true leader of today. Now think of yourself, you can be a student, a corporate guy or a homemaker, the simple rule is to learn to accept that there will be a hindrance in your way, you must strategize and plan beforehand and then win the battle called Life.

<u>3</u>

<u>IGNORANCE VERSUS DETERMINATION</u>

"Everyone you meet is fighting a battle, you know nothing about"- Wendy Mass

Identify and Hone your skills

We all know, how his skill with batting made him one of the renowned left-handed batsmen in the International cricket arena. But it can be said that he made a crucial contribution with his right-arm medium-pace bowling which was uncommon at that time. He could have evolved as an all-rounder if he had given an edge on his fielding. Though he took a hundred catches in the ODIs yet his concentration was to a great extent on batting.

Dada had the full potential of an all-rounder from the very beginning of his career. In the Lord's Test in 1996, he took three wickets with two in the initial innings and one in the second. It was at that match Ganguly could have emerged as an all-rounder even though the match was a draw. His medium pace in bowler-friendly weather gave the Indian Team an edge above. But soon after his debut series, he failed to focus on his bowling skills. Maybe because he had already made a mark as a batsman and his gentle medium-pace bowling was not the need of the time facing the Indian subcontinent ground which was more batsman-friendly. It can be stated that sheer ignorance towards his skill has left us from having an all-rounder among us. Surely so, as to how could he showcase his credibility as he didn't even bowl in twenty-one matches among the first thirty-three ODIs he played.

Though back in his home ground of Eden Garden during the 1997-98 season, he again made a valuable contribution as an all-rounder. In India's first innings against

Australia, he claimed three wickets including batsman Mark Taylor. We witnessed him as an all-rounder once again at the Sahara Cup against Pakistan in Toronto in 1997. He got recognition as both an outstanding batsman and an outstanding bowler. But this did not last for long. Over time, he was deemed as a batsman. We saw the deadly bowler again in the late years of his career under the captaincy of Kumble. He made a mesmerizing performance in the Feroz Shah Kotla stadium in the Test series against Pakistan.

Ganguly's potential as a true all-rounder was never really explored much. More concentration was given to his battling skills. Parallel to this is your situation. Yes, most of us get confused between our passion and profession and never pursue what is best for us. This is not only destructive for you but also damaging for those who you are working for. As you can never give your cent percent if you don't follow your heart. Trust me, never give up on your dreams, and let your skills to flourish. In such a situation, you would be able to give unconditional dedication to your work. And this will bring success to your life.

But I tell you, there are lucky few who can successfully align between this two. So most of them never care to hone their skillsets and do something opposite to their interest level. Therefore, first, get a clear picture of your interest or passion, then make a to-do list to achieve those. Don't worry so much about making money, you will make it if you are hardworking and dedicated enough.

Ganguly set another example when he pushed himself far ahead as a Captain of the Indian Cricket Team. Instead of developing on himself, he concentrated his full attention on preparing the teammates and look into the technicalities of the game also to bring the best factor out of them. Yes, this could be deemed as his exceptional quality to create genius players of tomorrow.

How he remained a good batsman and could have been better with his bowling if he had nurtured little more, teaches us never to give a blind eye to your skills. Yes, step by step you too can learn how to develop on your skills. Let me give you the basic framework for developing your skillsets.

-        First, know your passion or interest or your inclination

-        Then set to goal to achieve it within a deadline

-        Read books and articles to know more on your interest area

-        Find a mentor to guide you with your development

-        Maintain your individuality and don't shadow your mentor

-        Work on your weaknesses and stress on your strengths

-        Start finding a way to unleash it now or get a job related to it

-        Take vocational training or crash courses to further develop your skills

-        Learn recent developments in your interest area and keep on updating yourself

-        Act upon feedbacks and don't get agitated by negative remarks

These are a few ways by which you can easily work on your skills. But before everything else set a role model like Sourav Ganguly before you to motivate you throughout your journey towards the fulfilment of your dreams. He has already achieved his high standard and made a mark. His path could motivate you in this endeavor.

Just remember, mastering a skill will take you to the summit of success. So it's not an option in front of you, rather an imperative to strive harder towards your goal. But if you have two things in mind i.e., Fear and Procrastination habit you will never achieve your dream. You have to break free of the old shackles or myth that the only thing you need to do is to focus on earning money.

You have to be like Sourav, a true risk-taker. His career proved that. Nothing could stop him, he is unbeatable, unstoppable when came to his passion and love for the 22 yards game. He had partnered with some of the awesome teammates and created records that will remain in history. You too have to develop your skills and interest area into a professional expert level so that not only others will recognize it but also you will be happy and satisfied.

Life poses different sorts of challenges in front of us. We all like to escape the troubles. The winners always strive to break them and find out a path for all. That's the winner's choice, which has been Sourav Ganguly's choice. Now it's your turn. Nothing goes for waste, even if you fail in some of your initial endeavors, you will shine brighter in the coming days.

<u>**4**</u>

<u>CAPTAINCY AND BEYOND</u>

"If people are doubting how far you can go, go so far that you can't hear them anymore"- Michele Ruiz

Route to excellence

Captaincy did not come in handy for him. There was an instance during the Asian Test Championships, wherein his name came at the forefront of newspapers for vice-captaincy considering his performance in the last three years in the international platform. It was also confirmed by the selectors. But later, we found that Anil Kumble was appointed for the role. Here he learned the lesson on how to stay calm in the eyes of the storm.

Years later, when Sachin Tendulkar decided to quit his role as Captain of Indian Cricket Team, the situation was beyond control then. Match-fixing controversies had spread out so badly, that the Indian cricket scenario was about to tear apart. It was that time Sourav emerged as a Captain and a savior for which he was never credited. It was under his leadership the team got back into action. He took a new strategy to play it tough and aggressive competitive cricket and regain what they had lost. He brought harmony of understanding between the teammates including both senior and junior players.

The young Indian team member including Yuvraj Singh, Virender Sehwag, Harbhajan Singh, Zaheer Khan, and Mohammad Kaif looked up to him as their mentor. It was under his able leadership they became superstars of later years. Ganguly became another name for success. He began against South Africa in the home series and came out to be a winner. By that time season ended, the match-fixing scandal had surmounted and BCCI had to drop the players. So as the Captain, he had to choose a new team. A team that outplayed everyone from the beginning. Everyone recognized his ability as a true leader with his innovative strategies and concepts towards the game. A new concept of a foreign coach was introduced by him. It was that time Kiwi John Wright became the first Indian team coach and for the next five years, he along with Sourav Ganguly created the history of Indian cricket. The duo brought about a few changes in the fitness regime, sports medications, and psychotherapy. The team was ready to take up any challenge fighting against their opponents even on the home grounds. And these roaring tigers made their dream come true in the series against Australia in 2001 and 2003-04, at the 2003 World Cup in South Africa and 2004 in Pakistan.

He never lost faith in his choice of players. And we can say Dhoni was the product of this philosophy. Dhoni couldn't get a grip in the first four innings after is first ODI debut. But he made a fantastic turnaround to make 148 at Vishakhapatnam and then there was no looking back. The team and captain relationship grew stronger during this time. The NatWest final in 2002 saw another moment of passion and aggression when Ganguly stripped of his Indian Jersey and team India rouse to the summit of success.

Under his captaincy, the boys were not only fighting but also was enjoying it. He was so honest with his players, that his team trusted him blindly. He taught them to put the passion of the Nation before them and follow to the goal as if fighting for the nation. It was no less than a war having the same passion and emotion towards the country's victory. In the same manner, he captained the team for playing tests. He played nearly 49 tests series as a captain and India won 21 matches during his tenure.

Winning becomes a habit. So when you are leading something always put the interest of the organization in the foreground and have faith in your team members as this strategy will help to win over any challenge that might come your way. Never isolate your team and put yourself ahead, this is pure foolishness. Rather give time and effort in motivating youngsters and bring a bridge between the experienced and new team members.

Few steps to motivate your team players can be:

-	Set a clear and achievable goal

-	Sit and discuss with them if they need any clarification

-	Help them to prioritize work and don't put the excessive workload

-       Keep a positive and enthusiastic ambiance to encourage your team

-       Don't punish or complain against someone if he/she fails to achieve as per your order. Have faith

-       Keep an open forum where anyone can ask a question, listen to them and help them throughout to overcome them

-       Always organize employee-friendly training programs for the development of their skills and also learning new ones

-       Don't unnecessarily hover over their shoulder and scare the hell out of them

A positive atmosphere helps to achieve goals much faster than we can guess. A leader is the initiator of this positivity in the workplace. As this job of a team leader is new to you, am sure you are going to slip as many times as your predecessors. So don't worry, give time to yourself also to master the talent of nurturing a team.

It could be true to any professional, serving any profession or a student or a homemaker also. As a student, we are like a rudderless ship. We have only one ambition in life to be happy. Career comes much later in our mind, first and foremost our happiness stands tall. During this restless time also you must participate in different types of events, academic seminars, cultural events, college politics, sports. In doing each of this you need to be calculative just like

Ganguly. Quick and steady decisions come when you follow your idol and step ahead with the points mentioned ahead.

I could remember my college days at Scottish Church College, Kolkata. I was participating in an elocution contest where I had to perform with my team. I tried and could not motivate anyone, so I went ahead to recite the entire play alone. Everyone appreciated it but I was complete to failure to impress the judges. Because it was to judge my leadership skill also. That day another team won and performed at the cultural event named Calidonia. I was upset but I could understand I need a team and work with them. In later years, I became a filmmaker, but the learning from that day remained with me. Today I have a team that rely upon and also they look up to me. It's a mutual thing, it's about giving.

<u>5</u>

<u>GROWING CONTROVERSY</u>

"To be yourself in a world that is constantly trying to make you something else is the greatest accomplishment" - *Ralph Waldo Emerson*

Coping with the difficulties

On 20th May 2005 former Australian cricketer Greg Chappell was assigned the head coach of Team India. From the very beginning, the two were having tiffs. The highest point was at the Zimbabwe Tour in 2005 when Chappell commented on Ganguly's captaincy which the later handled very kindly. Followed by his elbow injury that prevented him to play in the Challenger Trophy. The dispute between the two rose so high that it started making news headlines. Then Greg Chappell sent an email to the BCCI stating that Ganguly was unfit physically and his divide and rule behavior is damaging the spirit of the Indian Team. The email got leaked and brought about huge protests and criticism from media, cricket fraternity, and mostly Ganguly's fans. To settle things the Board intervened and made attempts to bring them together. But due to the growing disputes with Chappell, Sourav dropped from the Team despite his good performance in the Test series. This was not taken in the good eye by the Kolkatans and they started protesting against the decision. People across the nation came forward to support the people of Kolkata.

The protest took a fierce figure when people started to block roads and railways and burn effigies of coach Chappell and selector Kiran More. There was a roar in the Parliament also asking for a valid answer from the then agriculture minister and BCC chief Sharad Pawar. Under pressure, BCCI selected Ganguly for the tour to Pakistan. Even though the team manager Raj Singh Dungarpur, who was not in favor of Ganguly, was asked to convince Greg Chappell to let Sourav Ganguly play.

Seemingly situations were under control. But the press made reports on the hidden fire between Ganguly and Chappell. Leading to this he got replaced by his deputy Rahul Dravid in November 2005. He was also dropped from the ODI team first, then the Test squad by the end of January 2006 just after the completion of the Karachi Test. Next six months we witnessed how Ganguly played hard to get runs at the domestic and county levels.

Meanwhile, there came a new turn of events. CAB Annual General Meeting and CAB official election were about to be organized. Dalmiya got elected over Prasun Mukherjee, then police commissioner. And Ganguly made a comeback thereafter. Sourav Ganguly, never hesitated for a moment to fight for the right. His confidence was the greatest virtues and dreaded by his opponents for this. Though he was surrounded by controversies, his conviction and clarity of thoughts helped him to handle any issue with cold head and led above all those. History will remember him for his captaincy and batting.

There was never pessimism in his attitude which is something to be learned. The dark chapter of his career might have a rivalry with Chappell. He was often called as Sourav 'Controversy' Ganguly due to hindrance in his path during his tenure. This is something worth learning.

You should always stay positive even when surrounded by negative people. How to do it is something to learn with the following pointers-

- Never get upset by them as you cannot do anything about it. Negativity is in the gene and it has nothing to do with you

- Stay away or maintain a mental distance from them while behaving cordially with them

- Even if that doesn't work, speak out to others, the most immediate person whom you can rely on. Let the other's know this

-Never give into negative talks. Just do what's right

- Stay grounded which helps you stay focus on your work and also stay present

- Think of how you can grow or learn something out of it

-Stay focused and work hard because the end of the day this will show

-Never be afraid to speak out against toxic people because it's due to them the entire environment is getting disturbed.

Mental peace is of the utmost importance when it comes to working in any place. Even if you are on Work from Home mode, you need a healthy ambiance around you.

Different things bother different persons. Sometimes unimportant issues make a person so concerned that he or she loses his patience. I remember my friend Anamika Sen, how happy she was while getting married. It was like a dream wedding for her were everything seemed right, and everybody supportive. Soon she had started complaining about her in-laws who were not ready to tolerate her career in modeling. She had to live with them only, then she learned to deal with it. She never pushed or pressurized her husband in any way. Rather made him aware of the situation. She focused on her career with more vigor and showed everyone that she can be productive as well. She gave them cold shoulder whenever they tried to manipulate her out of the profession. But again she did take good care of them and manipulate their emotions towards her.

Things are better now in her household. She also learned that life is no bed of roses. Yes, that is life. The sunny side of it is when you find peace and harmony in every hardship you put forth for work. It will come a day in your life when the negative people will also appreciate you. Bring out the best self of you and that's how you can go ahead in bringing your dreams to reality.

Remember, at the heart of any tiff lays a power struggle. Everyone wants to topple the other in the huddle race and come in the limelight. Sourav has an aura, an enigma that everyone feared. That might be the reason when many stepped in his path to ruin it. In his cricket career, there were 'N' number of controversies, which he tackled in the best way. Behind his calm and composed semblance lays an aggressive and driven soul which took him to the summit. He never feared anything or anyone. The most open-minded and outspoken person he is. The more you know, the more you will get influenced by his outstanding persona. Have at least from him, you can also succeed in your life and career.

<u>6</u>

<u>BIASED PRESS AND THE LEFT-HANDED</u>

<u>OFF-SIDE BATSMAN</u>

"Happiness is not something readymade. It comes

from your own actions

"- Dalai Lama XIV

Influencing beyond cricket

For some reason, Ganguly had created some haters in the Indian media houses who deliberately were maligning his stand. They tried to influence the opinions of a section of Indian cricket fans by being essentially regional in their nature. Forget about the Australian Media houses who ruthlessly publish unrealistic stories about the player. They were biased and nationalistic which was obvious as they never respected other teams except for their own. But what's wrong with Indian Media House like TOI, NDTV, and Cricinfos? They were spelling unrealistic stories about him and spreading hell lot of negativity around during September- December 2005. At that point, Sharad Pawar came forward and blamed the media for portraying Ganguly in the wrong manner. Though Rahul Dravid, the new captain of Team India kept mum during the entire episode which remained quite disturbing for us to accept. Rahul Dravid should have stood beside the right, that's the role of a captain when the player is in trouble. Though this situation was sympathized by Arjuna Ranatunga, Sri Lankan player, Wasim Akram, Pakistani Player. But behind all this one man's role should be questioned i.e., Greg Chappell who questioned Ganguly's integrity in the name of national player and cricket.

All this had affected Ganguly's batting badly. But he was aware of this and tried to get back in his form. But again his captaincy was questioned due to the Nagpur green-top episode against the Australian team. As he was alleged to have ducked the test in the name of a hand injury. Ganguly did submit the fitness report which clearly stated that he was suffering from tennis elbow by the team physio John Gloster. Yet the six-match ban imposed on him. The team was also losing its grip on the cricket field.

He never gave up in the eye of the storm. He tried to bring back the vigor of the team. He replaced himself from opening partnership with Sachin Tendulkar and paved the way for Sehwag in the greater interest of the Indian Team. He is definitely the most spirited sportsman of all time. There was a time when it was spread by the media that he is switching to politics. But he completed ignored these rumors, though he maintained his close proximity with Buddhadeb Bhattacharya and other CPI (M) leaders.

It was quite strange that the man who had scored 15,000 international runs was made to play domestics to prove his credibility. But here also Ganguly outshined others and got back his glory. Ganguly never spoke much rather he let his batting to do the miracle. And his actions evoked extreme reactions both positive and negative. The people went crazy when anything wrong said about him. They protested with full vigor. People across the nation prayed for this return and finally, the day came when he made his outstanding comeback.

This is so obvious in our lives. There are certain times when we feel the whole world is conspiring and we just can't give our cent percent to the work. This is human and quite normal. But we all have to come out of it and regain our productivity. Follow the effective steps to feel rejuvenated and refreshed:

-        First, cross out your previous to-do list because it's not working in your favor. Make a work-friendly list keeping in mind the time to be consumed in doing it. Make a sheet and keep a track of everyday progress. You can use colors that will keep it interesting all the more.

-        Keep a watch on your team that they are focussed on and staying as per the plan. This avoids delays and you all will complete the assignment just on time

-        Don't encourage too many unnecessary meetings with the teammates. Waste of time, rather chalk down their tasks in the initial meeting and then sit together once it is done

-       Always try to stay organized because it's the key to success. The doc/ excel/ ppt/ pdf etc., files should be named properly. Should be kept in a folder that is named on the project. Something like that.

-       Give priority to immediate tasks by maintaining a spreadsheet wherein each day's achievement is marked. This will move your project a step forward as you will be able to finish each task on that very day and you will also get to know how the work is progressing. You can add remarks also which will motivate the teammates

-        And what goes without saying, eat healthily and remain energized throughout the day. You can introduce snacks hour in the office wherein everyone will share and eat. This will help them to bond well and will fuel up their productivity.

-        Start exercising, begin with freehand and stretching exercises as it makes your body relaxed. Don't switch between day and evening exercises. Keep it consistent whenever and whatever you do

-        And most importantly keep your phone in silent mode. It's the social media surfing habit that takes away your productivity the most. Instead, you can take short breaks in between your work and take a brisk walk outside

Yup that the treat you give yourself to stay motivated and productive. Once you start, it becomes a habit and the system will operate accordingly. It is again applicable to each one of us. Be your own boss first, take control of all the bad habits, and get going with the above-mentioned points. Never ever others get the chance to put a finger on your credibility. If they do, keep calm and strive harder. Let your work say it for you, just like Sourav's.

It's tricky at times how people manipulate and dodge work and then the blame game starts. So it's up to you to be motivated and keep your team motivated. Because you cannot single-handed complete a work, need an able team to back you up. Master the quality of being a friendly boss, an understanding boss, and form an aura around you so that others can follow. Again just like Sourav, give way to juniors to flourish because making a bunch of followers is easy but bringing the leaders of tomorrow together is hard. So play the game, play it right.

7

TURNING THE WHEEL AROUND

"You don't have to be everyone's favourite, just be your own sunshine"- Dilip Kumar

The outstanding comeback in the International cricketing arena

Sourav was playing well in domestic cricket. During this time he worked on his techniques with tremendous determination and utmost focus. The middle of 2006, saw the fantastic comeback during the SA series at Johannesburg. After a long break of one year from the limelight, Ganguly bounced back in Team India, though as another team member. He was recalled after his middle-order replacements Suresh Raina and Mohammad Kaif suffered from poor form. At the warm-up match, he scored 83 against South Africa. In Potchefstroom, India won and Ganguly performed well. He caught the attention of observers who believed that Ganguly was in his best form, his strokes were positive and unafraid of the attacking bowling pattern of the opponents. Ganguly's performance lifted the spirit of the Team again. Ganguly and Sreesanth played a pivotal role behind the winning of the match after so many years.

He was making a mark as a successful batsman for India in the next test series. He played a crucial role in the Indian dressing room and also acted as a morale booster with his experience down the line. It was Ganguly who emerged as a true leader and silenced all his critics in due course. He proved himself once again in the innings at Johannesburg.

But this was not enough, as everybody was waiting for his comeback in the ODIs. During this time, the national selectors chaired by Dilip Vensarkar announced the squad for the first two ODIs against West Indies and a preliminary thirty-member squad for ICC World Cup in West Indies, March 2007. Kumble, Sehwag, and Irfan Pathan were left out of it and eventually, Ganguly found a place in the fifteen-member squad for the first two ODIs against West Indies.

It was a great opportunity for Ganguly to have played ODI again after fifteen months of gap. He was scoring high and the team was winning back-to-back ODI tournaments. Soon thereafter Ganguly was made a part of the World Cup 2007 squad. The wheel had finally turned around in Ganguly's favor. Ganguly played his best and major came to be known for his majestic stroke play with off-side touch and cover drive. His killer instinct he had just nailed it. Everyone from Sunil Gavaskar, Brian Lara, Geoffrey Boycott, Arjuna

Ranatunga praised him for his aggression. They came forward to speak in favor of him and clearly stated that it was a wrong decision to have kept Ganguly out of the Indian team.

The year 2007 saw the change in form of Indian cricket. The country returned to its winning mode in all forms of cricket including the T20s. From here we can draw that his confrontation with coach Chappell was really unfortunate but it gave him the impetus to fight back and emerge as a winner.

So in a situation of utmost disorder, whenever is beyond your control just do like Sourav Ganguly. His passion for cricket took him on. He, who never gave up on anything became our icon for generations.

The idea is to keep fighting in the face of failure. How to do so is the question in your mind right now. Let me make it simple with the following steps:

-         First and foremost, be honest with your superiors. Do inform them what had gone wrong, when, how, and where it got failed. In addition, make homework on explaining the strategies you think should help in overcoming this situation. This will not only take off the pressure from your shoulder but also get you in the right light in front of them.

-        Use the very emotion of being a failure to make you stronger. Over the years we are taught success is the only route to getting ahead in life. No, it's absolutely wrong. Because only when you fail, you know the true value for your goal and you bounce back. So take it positively and find out a way to set things right by learning from your mistakes

-        Take in other's opinions and feedback. Don't sway out of it or avoid it to get hurt. Remember it's not personal rather it's for the good of the organization you work. So have patience and humility and open up for fresh confrontations or discussions on your performance

-        Find out the opportunities to explore new avenues instead of toiling with the same strategy which is just not working. Suppose you have made a great research and hard work in developing an app. But it's not working among the targeted people. Go ahead and take their feedback and find out what they expected out of it and where have you gone wrong. Master the ability to handle a lot many things at a time.

-       Just don't give up at any point. At the wee hour take on to a new project and make it successful based on your learning from the previous one. Show your determination to your superiors and strategize well to create an impression on them. And once you are assigned on a new project, just show it.

-       Remember, you are not alone. You have an entire team to support you. Steer them in the right direction and motivate them throughout.

This is the best and perhaps the only way to tackle failure and get is out of your system. Unfortunately, you will have multiple failures in your life both personal and professional. Just play the winning shot by being your best. If you are honest and dedicated to your work, you will definitely bounce back from your failures.

Most people refuse to accept their failure and they become hostile when confronted. They must stop fooling themselves and find out the thousand best ways to bring back the lost glory. And eventually out of the thousand, one will work in your favor. And when you reach your goal don't forget to pamper yourself. Because it's you who wears the cap on his or her head. Reward yourself in achieving your goal of succeeding in your work.

<u>8</u>

<u>EMBRACING THE NEW ROLES, NEW PLATFORMS</u>

"The secret of getting ahead, is getting started" -

Mark Twain

Retirement and life beyond

Sourav Ganguly announced his retirement from international cricket at a press conference called on 7th October 2008. It was Durga Ashtami that day when the whole of Indian especially Bengal doomed to sadness. His cricket fans were unhappy because they will never see him again wearing the cap of the Indian team again. His decision was out of dismay when he was kept out of some crucial game like Irani Trophy. This was clearly a humiliation which he was not ready to take. So despite being in good form he did call it a day.

In 2008, at the inaugural edition of IPL, he was one of the icon players. Our Maharaj was the captain of the Kolkata Knight Rider, the franchise that was owned by Bollywood Superstar Shah Rukh Khan. They two had a bonding instantly. Shah Rukh Khan with his surmounts energy, ready wit, and outstanding personality could easily befriend the master cricket player. Together they created history once more.

During this time Sourav got appointed as the host of the reality quiz show Dadagiri Unlimited by Zee Bangla Television. The show had an innovative format wherein participants represented 19 districts of West Bengal, who had to answer the questions presented by Ganguly. We saw a new angle of the hero wherein he helped people coming from far zillas to speak about their achievement. The platform came as a motivation for others. He was then got appointed as the chairman of CAB's Cricket Development Committee. The basic idea was to make the selectors accountable after every cricket session and make necessary recommendations and changes.

He was always on the right track. He again played Ranji Cup in the Bengal team, in October 2009. Brendon McCullum was there selected to lead the KKR Team that year. He again returned as the captain of KKR in 2010. People were rejoicing to see him on the cricket ground in full form. Again, 2011 he was signed by Pune Warriors. Though he played for the next two seasons, he decided to take a break. He took retirement from IPL making a formal announcement on 29th October 2012.

Post his retirement he got involved in the development of the team. In the year 2019, the BCCI saw a new president, our Maharaj i.e., Sourav Ganguly chaired the position. His contributions to sports are countless. And thus he was awarded for his outstanding contribution in the field of sports. Some are Sports star Person of the Year, Arjuna Award, CEAT Indian Captain of the Year, Padma Shri in 2004, Rammohan Roy Award. On 20th May 2013 Government of West Bengal honored him with Banga Bibhusan Award.

Today, we get so attached to a job we often forget to explore the options. There may be thousands of options open in front of you just waiting for your awakening. But choosing the best option is where your credibility lay in. Let me explain this:

-          Take a rational decision in choosing that job which will give you job satisfaction. Find out the credentials needed for it and then check if you have the drive in you to go ahead with it. Often you get a job having zero experience and a person having fifteen years toiling experience fails to impress the recruiters. This is where they fail, they are not ready to experiment with new things

-          Analyse the progress path of the company. Do a little research on the company before you join or appear for an interview. Find out how the employees are encouraged, if there is learning/training scope, proper appraisal policies, the salary package, and most importantly the ambiance, authority to take decisions, autonomy versus supervision.

-       So far you have looked into the role and the company, but it's time now to find out how to fit it is for you. Find out whether this will serve your objective. And most importantly, find out whether it will give you a sense of fulfilment. Otherwise, there is no pointing change to a new role or job.

It's a very important decision on your part to leave a job role and start off with a new one. Take your time and analyse each aspect deeply. If you are supercharged up to make this shift in your career, go ahead and strike the right chord. If applies to people who also take voluntary retirement. Don't just sit back and think the game is over. Maybe this is the time to start over afresh.

There are countless times we leave options and just let it go because of our lethargy. So to energize yourself do some reading. May be a book of someone you idealize, someone like Sourav Ganguly whose entire life is just like a lesson to learn from. I know it's often too hard to objectify human emotions and inclinations. But the key is to search, search, and search what fits for you.

Initially when my father retired from his job, he use to do nothing. Then one day I saw him cutting interesting articles on sports from the newspaper. He added it to his notebook and made his own remark. I introduced him to Twitter, and that day he found a new world opened in front of him. He started writing at every scope and opportunity came when he was getting job offers to writer in freelancing sites. And that's how it all started.

This is just another personal experience I am sharing with you to motivate you and give direction to your rudderless ship. If you are not happy doing something, some work or jobs it's clearly a signal to make a shift. As change is always for good. Even if you fail at any attempt, remember Ganguly how he never loses his calm. He realized his drawback and worked on his skills and then think about his comeback in the team. Generations after generations will remember how hard he played, and how rightly he played. He always brought newness to the sports. Just like he introduced the pink ball and thus welcoming the new for tomorrow's cricketers. He is our Dada posing extreme dadagiri whenever and wherever the situation went adverse.

<u>9</u>

<u>THINK LIKE SOURAV, THINK OF SUCCESS</u>

"All our dreams can come true, if we have the courage to pursue them" - *Walt Disney*

Association with brands

Ganguly had created a strong image by means of his outstanding sportsmanship. The famous off drives and towering sixes made him an indispensable entity for cricket. In fact, he is the best left-handed batsman India has produced. His captaincy was also successful. He had by then created an image for himself. Not just as an aggressive professional player with great determination but also a great team player. People just loved his elegance and style.

This image essentially increased Ganguly's brand equity. Sourav became a brand resembling fighters with his comeback in 2007. The most popular advertisement was the emotional Pepsi ad which announced his comeback with the caption: *'Hope you have not forgotten me'*. During this time Ganguly got into the contract as Brand Ambassador with German-based sports lifestyle brand Puma and Puma India. Then, with Chirag Computers, a Kolkata based IT Hardware concern. In the mid of 2007, he was roped in as Brand Ambassador of Captain TMT which became quite popular with its aggressive stance. Sourav Ganguly then came into association with some other brands like Hero Honda, Sahara, Pepsi, Lupin Pharma, and Tata Teleservices. Again in 2008, he became Brand Ambassador of INX News. He started to bond more with the public with a show at NewsX.

This immense Brand Value off-field was an exception. Actually, in a diversified country where unity matters a lot, Brand Ganguly was an automatic choice. This because under his leadership we found the most incredible bonding of players and formation of 'Team India'. And his presence was so strong, that we saw how the crowd at Wanderers and Cape Town screamed- *'Daaada Daaada'* just like any other Indian fans at his comeback.

Sports in any country do not essentially mean victory, medals, and trophies. It's also an emotional bonding with the sports and the sportsman. Sourav Ganguly is not a name anymore, it's a sentiment and a feeling of struggle and winning after the huge agony and pain. And for Kolkata, when suddenly a young man appeared on the international platform, such a matter of great pride. Kolkatans loved this rebellion youth and in him, they found their Dada or Elder Brother.

Now if you are thinking, the only successful person has an image and for the rest, it's just a bit overwhelming. Then you are wrong. Even as at a leadership position or as a new entrepreneur you need to develop your own image. You can make people, precise your customers talk about you by simply following the rules of Image Building:

-        First, recognize your true strength i.e., that something which makes you different from others. People want to know the real you, so dig into your soul and discover your talent

-        Make it a point that you will never leave your personal image branding task aside. It's a perpetual exercise and you have to be attached to it on regular basis. Make it your habit

-        Thereafter, start working on a Blog that establishes your personal brand by reaching out to the audiences. But don't just start a blog and forget about it. Rather built on it and give more power to it

-        All the content you provide should have the power to attract the audience. So make it a mix of different formats. And adding to its look, install a great design that would be smart and classy. As this will reflect your persona

-        Interact with your followers as this is the new age rule. Otherwise, they will doom you to be arrogant and may leave you aside. Be a people's person and in due course inspire them with your experience based stories

-        Get yourself associated with voluntary activities. Connect to people and help them with their mission. Like education and health for both child and elderly persons are a concern for all of us. Join hand with some groups serving them during this corona phase

-        Make an account on professional platforms and learn to flourish yourself and your business via it. For example, LinkedIn is the best platform for branding and unfolding yourself

-        Network with professionals of your arena on social media all across the globe. Explore this opportunity to connect with your audience also. Communicate your audience and ask them their story and tell them how relatable those are or inspiring for others. This was you can connect with millions

- You can only go a step ahead by organizing an event and use that podium to speak out on your subject of expertise. Let others talk and listen to them. Mutual adulation is a part of the strategy. It's like the Tagore song: 'Amra sobai raja, amader ei rajar rajyotye'.

- Have a website of your own to represent your body of work. Developing it take the advice of experts in writing, designing, and developing it. It is the boss of personal branding, so be very careful

- Now what you have to do is to keep on examining your progress. Use Google Analytics or any other tool to do so. Or simply you can Google your name and find out how people perceive you. Then work on further polishing it

-        Never lose your enthusiasm at any point in time. Because sometimes it could be a long process to establish yourself as a successful brand. Motivate yourself, podcast, or just sing out loud to relax and rejuvenate.

Think about how Sourav made it to the top. How he fought back each time. That's the only route to success. I have heard people saying that they couldn't achieve such and such thing due to backbiting or politics at the workplace. To them I can say, it's an inevitable part of our life now. Be just cannot avoid these. But if they are wrong, show it to them that you are right. Speak up wherever necessary. And also remained determined to your activities and let your work speak on your behalf.

Leave aside all negativity. It's like a phone call if you don't like to talk just disconnect it. The button is in your hand. Whenever your image is feeling challenged, make a point to set it right.

<u>10</u>

<u>THE CONCLUSION</u>

"It's hard to beat a person who never gives up" -

Babe Ruth

Lessons drawn from his life

Recall the era of Indian cricket from 2002-2008, you will indulge in a unique emotion named Sourav Ganguly. His entire journey on and off the cricket field has been an inspiration. You will be thrilled and motivate reading through each chapter, and draw a lesson out of it.

Though he retired in 2008 from International cricket people never stop to love him. Here are some moments of his glory:

- He was a determined player from the very beginning. Though he dropped initially alleging to have an arrogant attitude. He came back with more vigor in his strokes

- Took up the captaincy of Indian Team when the players were allegedly blamed in the match-fixing scandal

- He changed the dimension of Indian cricket by introducing aggression in the team

- He led the team to victory in the overseas ground. Earlier they were hardly any victory in the foreign grounds.

- He brought about a team spirit and built future leaders like Laxman, Kumble, Harbhajan, Sehwag, Zaheer, Yubraj, and Dhoni. He groomed them to become what they are today

- He went beyond regionalism in the team selection for the first time. He incorporated the idea of Team India and nurtured it.

- In the big match at Lords, he took his jersey off and swing it in the air as a symbol of joy and victory. He showed Indian cricketers are equally aggressive like other international teams

- Though no World Cups were won, yet he won millions of hearts. Who can forget the World Cup 2003, wherein reaching at the finals with such a young team was much credited

- His retirement was the shock in between the puja for Bengalis and the people of the entire nation

- Still today his witty comment from the commentary box entertains us no less. He is very fluent in English and his commentary is one of the best things in every recent match. People feel energetic whenever they hear his beautiful voice.

-        Even in the show Dadagiri Unlimited, he uplifted many people and became a source of inspiration for all people

-        Sourav Ganguly Cricket School which is incorporated under the Government of India, Ministry of Corporate Affairs strives for cricketers of tomorrow. The cricket clinic, which is the brainchild of Sourav himself, not only hone cricketing skills but of the holistic development of the students. The school will bring some of the finest cricketers in the coming years.

Sourav Ganguly, or as we call him Dada is not only a cricketer. He is an inspiration for many things like standing high with your principle keeping intact your self-belief, always come back and not to quit at any adverse situation, instilling belief in others that they can also do it, leadership, and team player instinct.

Everyone loves him. He is everyone's favorite Dada. How an enigma turned to be a household's name is something we learned throughout the book. He taught too many things and most importantly how to remain driven in our life even in the time of Corona. He has been in home isolation for over a week after his elder brother, Snehasish Ganguly, was tested positive with the highly contagious virus. He promised his followers that he will come back soon. He is now back with his killer instinct driving us all ahead.

The young man with his ruthless aggression had won the million hearts. Now the mature man takes up more responsibilities as President of BCCI. He is setting the road map of Team India. He was always against regionalism. He once mockingly said- *'The entire ground belongs to me'*. He represents the Fearless and Fabulous India in front of the rest of the world.

While reading through the chapter we got an elaborate idea on the following:-

-       We learned how to be disciplined, keeping up with our principles

-       We learned how to remain true to our goals

-       We learned how to tackle negative people

-       We learned how to bounce back after a failure

-       We learned how to motivate our team members

-       We learned how to build our personal image

I have also shown how this learning can be appropriate for us also. And given some amazing hacks to get going with your dreams. You have to chase your dreams to make it a reality.

Each one of us go through some amount of ups and downs, all of you do because that is life. You will learn ways to handle such situations. Don't get stressed out on your goals because it's your dream, it's your chance and it's you who have to make it happen. Dada, as diehard fans around the world, even then he had to face so many obstacles throughout his career. Not a single moment he rested, not a single moment he had cried. He often says that the tears are an easy escape for the weak.

There is no harm in learning from others especially from someone like Sourav Ganguly. This iconic man never stopped at any point. He never looked back to repent any of his decision. I wish I had the chance to hear his journey from him only. Like many, I too wish to meet him someday. But for now, my research and my insightful analysis of his life along with the tips to apply in your life will intrigue you.

Are you really feeling tired and demotivated in your life? Nothing seems to interest you? Are you scared to face the big challenges at your workplace or home? Then I have an answer for you are. Go ahead and read each chapter a thousand times, you will learn to say 'NO' to your lethargy. This is perhaps the only way to be happy in life and career. I focused a lot on his career and some little on his life in this writing. Because efficiency was proved with his work. I would, therefore, emphasize Dona Ganguly, his wife, and Sana Ganguly, his daughter are just as proud of him as we are.